The Gifts of Divorce

A Workbook for Healing & Self-Discovery

JAMIE DANIEL, MS, LMFT

BALBOA
PRESS
A DIVISION OF HAY HOUSE

Cover Illustration by Joan Perrin-Falquet

Balboa Press books may be ordered through booksellers or by contacting:

Balboa Press
A Division of Hay House
1663 Liberty Drive
Bloomington, IN 47403
www.balboapress.com
1 (877) 407-4847

Print information available on the last page.

ISBN: 978-1-5043-6118-7 (sc)
ISBN: 978-1-5043-6119-4 (e)

Balboa Press rev. date: 08/24/2016

DEDICATION

This workbook is dedicated to all the brave hearts,
the survivors of divorce and loss.
Never forget your value, your worth, and your
amazing strength and courage.

CONTENTS

THE GIFTS OF DIVORCE

The idea of divorce as a process capable of bearing gifts may seem counterintuitive. After all, many of us experience divorce as a tremendous loss. It's a wrenching apart of souls that were formerly joined, the removal of one from another, a disentangling of lives with intertwining roots.

Yet everything that happens in life contains the seed of a potential gift, as do the people in our lives — our parents, partners, children. Each of them is a teacher, holding up a mirror, bringing gifts in the form of lessons, and all playing an integral part in our journey.

By definition a gift possesses a special ability, power, quality, or attribute, so as you begin to reflect on your journey in the pages of this workbook, ask yourself, *How is the experience of divorce empowering me? Am I beginning to see qualities and attributes in myself that I hadn't noticed before?*

While divorce is seldom easy, the gifts it confers can be extremely rewarding. Here are just a few I've chosen to highlight:

THE GIFT OF A BEGINNER'S MIND

As you embark on the journey of divorce recovery, empower yourself with the gift of a beginner's mind. A beginner's mind awards you a fresh pair of eyes. Like a young child seeing things for the first time, new thoughts and ideas will flow into your experience.

You're in the process of writing a brand new chapter in your life. With a beginner's mind, all past perceptions and self-judgments are released. You view yourself, your life, and all the endless possibilities before you without bias or limitation. You explore new ideas, hone your vision, and realize a new life that is better aligned with who you are.

Walking the path of self-discovery with a beginner's mind allows you to enter new relationships with a clearer perception of what you want and deserve. You work hard to let go of past resentments in order not to bring them into future relationships. Self-respect is your compass as you learn to define yourself in new ways.

THE GIFT OF NONJUDGMENT

Practicing a technique called mindfulness will enhance your ability to keep an open mind. With an open mind, you can learn not to judge yourself or others, but rather to simply notice what you are thinking and feeling, and, at the same time, exercise self-compassion for these thoughts and feelings.

Divorce is rife with challenges. There's so much to reckon with, it helps you develop a new appreciation and compassion for others who face challenges in their lives. As part of humanity, we're all imperfect beings, learning lessons along the way. When you can listen to and support others right where they are, without judgment, you allow them, and yourself, the opportunity to be real.

Taking personal responsibility for your actions, and exercising self-compassion along the way, allows self-judgment to fall away. Only when you learn to accept yourself with all your imperfections can you fully accept another.

THE GIFT OF FEELING ALIVE

Mindfulness reminds you that your breath is your anchor. It has been with you since birth and is still by your side. Practicing mindfulness will heighten your awareness to your senses of sight, sound, taste, smell, and touch. You may be gifted with feeling more alive than you have in a long time.

Feeling alive again can send you on a wondrous journey to discover your new passions in life. *What excites you? What have you always wanted to do or try? What foods do you love? What makes your heart sing?* These are important questions worthy of your time and attention.

With a beginner's mind, you can become a student of life again. You have a new openness and curiosity that is fully alive and aware. If you experienced a feeling of numbness before your divorce, you no longer will. Though some emotions are intensely painful as we heal, the joys are also intensely joyful. You can develop a new appreciation and gratitude for the people and situations in your life.

THE GIFT OF COMMUNITY

The experience of divorce can promote the seeking out of meaningful friendships, associations, and areas of interest for self-growth. You may notice like-minded people suddenly gravitating toward you, such as other women who are going through a divorce. You may become fast friends and ardent supporters of each other during a difficult passage in your lives.

You may also be healed by the opportunity to help others in need. Whether through volunteering, or supporting friends who are going through personal hardships of their own, you'll have a new appreciation for helping those in need. It is very healing to offer small gestures of kindness to others.

You may join groups, clubs, or causes that cover topics or activities of interest to you. Opening new doors in your life will lead to another new door. The gift of community opens your world to new and exciting opportunities and adventures.

THE GIFT OF FRIENDSHIPS

Over your lifetime, friends will come in and out of your circle. During divorce, you may feel judged and misunderstood by family members, children, or old friends. This can be both painful and isolating. Those who've not experienced divorce sometimes have a difficult time putting themselves in your shoes, and, frankly, it scares them. "If *she's* getting a divorce, could it happen to me?"

Having a tribe of supportive friends can be a source of centering and healing. I'm speaking about friends who accept you as you are, love you through your journey, and are there to offer their honest advice if you need a sounding board.

Finding a tribe of healthy, supportive friends, united by this common experience, is one of the most valuable gifts of divorce. Knowing you are not alone on your journey, being able to be your authentic self and not be judged, and having others with whom to share laughter and tears as you go along is priceless.

Friends are gems and treasures to be cherished!

THE GIFT OF DESIGNING A LIFE
OF YOUR OWN CREATION

If you are divorcing at mid-life after a decades long marriage, it's likely your life was defined by the important roles you played: wife, mother, homemaker, soccer mom, room mother, volunteer and so on. One incredible gift of divorce is that you're now in a position to design a life that speaks authentically and meaningfully to you - a life that represents your unique purpose, values, and talents.

Marriage has a way of muting your individuality, eventually blurring the lines between "me" and "we." Becoming a parent creates an even further distance between you as a wife and mother, and you as a unique individual in the world. Divorce at mid-life affords you the opportunity to reacquaint yourself with the unique individual that you are and the life you want to manifest as that individual.

Enjoy this amazing part of your journey. If you've forgotten who you are after years of focusing your attention on your family, now is the time you get to rediscover yourself. Try new things, have new adventures, identify what matters most to you now. It's never too late to go back to school, choose a different career and walk down a new path.

What are the whispers of your heart? What makes your soul light up? What passions burn fires under you?

THE GIFT OF SELF-DISCOVERY

Self-discovery is the biggest gift of all. The experience of divorce can be a platform for truly seeing, accepting, acknowledging, and loving who you are, being able to claim your imperfections, strengths, and talents with loving acceptance and confidence, and fully owning and appreciating your unique individual beauty. This is your time to live and manifest a life that is about your values and dreams, a life full of self-respect and gratitude for what it took you to get here.

All of these gifts are earned and have positive lifelong impact. As you begin down the road to self-discovery, put on your beginner's eyes, quiet the voice of self-judgment, and meet yourself for the first time.

CHILDHOOD, MARRIAGE & YOUR OLD CORE BELIEFS

I recently came across the word, *metanoia*. Metanoia is of Greek origin, meaning "the journey of changing one's mind, heart, self or way of life." That certainly can describe one's experience of divorce, and more importantly, of the healing that can take place in terms of one's view of their value and self-worth.

HOW YOUR CHILDHOOD & YOUR MARRIAGE INTERSECT

When you were born, you were a beautiful, blank canvas. You inherited a genetic predisposition to certain biological, psychological and sociological tendencies, and you were born with a particular temperament. After that, you were like a sponge absorbing and forming important beliefs about yourself based on familial and cultural messages. There were important figures in your life instilling and reinforcing those beliefs – parents, teachers, mentors, peers – and eventually you yourself began to reinforce them by choosing your experiences and viewing them through the lens of your beliefs about yourself and the world. This is better illustrated in the following case of Sally.

THE CASE OF SALLY

Sally was born the last of five children to hard-working parents. Her parents were older when she was born and they had limited time and personal resources for Sally. One message that Sally and her siblings had been taught was that "children are to be seen and not heard," so they silenced their voices and communicated little to their parents. Her father suffered from alcoholism for several years. During her childhood there was so much turmoil in the home, Sally decided not to add any drama of her own. She did everything she could to please and help keep the peace. Her parents reinforced the belief that Sally was a good child. Sally learned that she could receive love as long as she was being "good."

When Sally grew up, she married a man who was emotionally unavailable. He suffered from an addiction and this became a family secret. Sally's experience was that she and her husband rarely had meaningful conversations, and he seldom asked her about her day. There were many occasions when Sally felt extremely hurt and disrespected by her husband when he would ogle other women in public in front of her, even after she had repeatedly told him how hurtful this was. Sally was married for 28 years before her husband's addiction issues and hurtful behaviors contributed to the end of their marriage.

During Sally's divorce she felt her self-worth was at rock bottom. She believed that if she stood up for herself she wasn't being viewed as "good" and worried that by getting a divorce she would lose the love of her family. Sally's voice had been silenced for what seemed her entire life. Now she was beginning to speak and tell the family about the truth of her marriage.

Sally has many old core beliefs. Can you guess what they are? A few of them are that she believes she is unimportant, unworthy of time and attention, and that she did not really matter to anyone. These beliefs began in childhood and were reinforced in her marriage. Sally's divorce provided her an opportunity to see where she needed to heal and grow in her life. Sally began to challenge her old beliefs about herself and slowly replace them with more accurate and positive self-beliefs.

WHAT ARE YOUR OLD CORE BELIEFS?

It's important that you take some time to identify your old core beliefs about yourself. As you do that, briefly revisit your childhood to see where you began to form those beliefs. As you grew older and eventually married you took those beliefs with you. They played an important role in your choice of partner and in the dynamics in your marriage.

In order to heal and have the ability to form healthier relationships with yourself and others in the future, you need to identify and challenge your old core beliefs about yourself.

What are some old beliefs you hold about yourself? On the following page, take a few minutes to see if you can identify some of them.

MY OLD CORE BELIEFS ABOUT MYSELF ARE:

MY STORY & INSPIRATION

My divorce took fifteen months. We went through mediation, and the procedure was very civil. The emotional fallout was anything but. It felt as though judgment and condemnation came at me from all sides. It was overwhelming. Looking back, I wonder how much of the condemnation was my own.

That was the beginning of my journey toward healing and recovery from divorce. I was fifty years old and starting my life all over again, confronted with so many questions, fears, and anxieties, all while coping with tremendous grief. Add to this the problem of low self-esteem, and it's easy to find oneself lost.

Looking back, I don't think I knew how lost I was. You could ask me anything at all about my children or my husband, and I knew the answer. But when the subject was me, I came up blank. *Who am I?* I didn't know. *Do I matter?* I wasn't sure. *Will anyone ever love me?* I was certain they wouldn't. *What is my worth?* It felt at zero. *How will I support myself? What am I good at?* ... and on and on.

Like many, my journey toward healing was painful, slow and steady. My goal was to be able to answer the questions above. The next two years were spent reacquainting myself with the "me" who'd been forgotten or misplaced along the way. I relied on prayer, self-help books, and sessions with my therapist, along with hours of self-reflection. I had to learn many things the hard way, but learn them I did.

As the first few transformative years were happening, my oldest son's marriage was celebrated, followed by the birth of my first grandchild. There were so many life transitions, and I was a mother who did her best to get through them with few personal resources.

Three years after the divorce, I had a light-bulb moment. After much prayer over what career to pursue after twenty-plus years of being a stay-at-home mom, it hit me: I wanted to be a therapist and help others through the painful process of divorce recovery. I felt there weren't enough resources in the community, and I wanted to be part of that change. I got my master's degree in clinical counseling after two years of study. After four years of a post-graduate internship I became licensed and opened my private practice.

I consider mine a success story. You truly can do anything you set your mind to, no matter your age, no matter the past limitations you may have imposed on yourself. When you open your mind and fully realize your strengths and character, you can do anything. The sky's the limit!

MY GIFT TO YOU

The road to divorce recovery is a winding one, with many twists and turns and ups and downs. Along the way you'll experience joy and sorrow, doubt and clarity, amazing adventures and difficult lessons — all a part of your higher self's journey toward growth and healing.

Divorce can challenge the very core of your self-worth. This makes the journey traveled inward, exploring your inner self, an important part of recovery. Self-reflection leads to self-discovery, reuniting you with your true essence. As you rediscover who you truly are — learning from your past and beginning to set goals and a vision for what you want to manifest in your life — you're on the path to building an amazing life.

I wrote this workbook and the healing affirmations expressly for those of you going through a divorce. I centered them around your most vulnerable questions and uncertainties. I seek to help empower you with the wisdom you may not yet see within yourself, to provide comfort and reassurance when you need it most. The answers you are seeking are there. It just takes self-reflection to access them.

My prayer for you is that you begin your own journey with an open mind, a tender heart, an unbridled self, and a new love of life.

HOW TO USE THIS WORKBOOK

The power of affirmations to heal and transform your life is what this workbook seeks to promote. Keep it beside your bed for easy reference. On happy days, and on difficult days, open it and see which affirmation comes up for you. I've included reflection pages after each affirmation, and at the end of the book, to encourage the process of reconnecting with your authentic self. Taking a moment to write and reflect on these pages will help you uncover, and ultimately celebrate, the beauty and splendor of who you truly are, placing you that much further down the road to healing and transformation.

As you do so, always, always remember — You are loved.

AFFIRMATIONS TO HEAL & TRANSFORM YOUR LIFE

The most beautiful people we have known are those who have known defeat, known suffering, known struggle, known loss, and have found their way out of the depths. These persons have an appreciation, sensitivity, and an understanding of life that fills them with compassion, gentleness, and a deep loving concern. Beautiful people do not just happen.

~ Elizabeth Kubler Ross

1. YOU ARE BEAUTIFUL

Like the caterpillar that must painfully squeeze through the cocoon in order to realize its most beautiful potential, so goes your journey. From darkness to light, you spread your wings.
You are beautiful.

ASPECTS OF MY BEAUTY I HAD FORGOTTEN ARE

AS I LEARN TO APPRECIATE MY ESSENCE I CAN

You can be the most beautiful person in the world and everybody sees light and rainbows when they look at you, but if you yourself don't know it, all of that doesn't even matter. Every second that you spend on doubting your worth, every moment that you use to criticize yourself is a second of your life wasted, is a moment of your life thrown away. It's not like you have forever, so don't waste any of your seconds, don't throw even one of your moments away.

~ C. Joybell C.

2. YOU ARE WORTHY

Just as you are in this moment.
As a child of God and the Universe.
For being unique in your journey and being.
Of all good and true things.
Of kindness, respect, and love.
You are worthy.

I AM ADMIRED FOR MY

AS I EMBRACE MY WORTHINESS, I DESERVE

I have come to accept the feeling of not knowing where I am going. And I have trained myself to love it. Because it is only when we are suspended in mid-air with no landing in sight, that we force our wings to unravel and alas begin our flight. And as we fly, we still may not know where we are going. But the miracle is in the unfolding of the wings. You may not know where you're going, but you know that so long as you spread your wings, the winds will carry you.

~ C. JoyBell C.

3. YOU ARE EXACTLY WHERE YOU ARE MEANT TO BE

Amidst the confusion, the self-doubt, and feeling
lost, know that the Universe has put you right
here, right now. There is a lesson to be learned
in order for your higher self to achieve its
greatest potential. Your purpose will unfold.
You are exactly where you are meant
to be.

AS I GRIEVE WHAT WAS, I BEGIN TO
UNDERSTAND THAT

AS I STRUGGLE TO FEEL COMFORTABLE
WITH THE UNKNOWN, I TRUST THAT

Never forget that once upon a time, in an unguarded moment, you recognized yourself as a friend.

~ Elizabeth Gilbert

4. YOU WILL BE OKAY

After the darkness comes the
dawn. After winter comes
spring. Out of every ending
comes a new beginning. You
have survived many challenges.
You will be okay.

CHALLENGES I HAVE SURVIVED IN MY PAST ARE

I WILL BE OKAY BECAUSE I KNOW THAT

Your perspective on life comes from the
cage you were held captive in.

~ Shannon L. Alder

5. YOU ARE A FIGHTER

For all that is true and meaningful.
For your newfound clarity.
For your values and principles.
For your self-respect and reclaimed soul.
As you fight for the ability to accept and
let go, you celebrate the freedom
to live an authentic life.
You are a fighter.

MY VALUES AND PRINCIPLES INCLUDE

SELF-RESPECT IN MY LIFE LOOKS LIKE

If you could kick the person in the pants responsible for most of your trouble, you wouldn't sit for a month.

~ Theodore Roosevelt

6. YOU ACCEPT RESPONSIBILITY

For your part in the relationship's ending.
To exercise self-compassion along the way.
To understand there are no failures, only lessons.
To build a healthy support system in your life.
To stand on your own two feet.
For understanding no one can rescue you.
To always be your own hero.
With love, you accept responsibility.

I TAKE RESPONSIBILITY FOR

I EXERCISE SELF-COMPASSION BY
UNDERSTANDING THAT

Bran thought about it. "Can a man still
be brave if he's afraid?"
"That is the only time a man can be brave,"
his father told him.

~ George R.R. Martin
A Game of Thrones

7. YOU ARE BRAVE

For your strong heart and determination.
For listening to your inner voice.
As you stand and face adversity.
For sharing your truth with others.
For making it through, day-by-day.
For trusting in a future of your creation.
You are incredibly brave.

I AM DETERMINED TO

THE ADVERSITY I FACE IS

Someday you're gonna look back on this moment
of your life as such a sweet time of grieving.
You'll see that you were in mourning and your
heart was broken, but your life was changing....

~ Elizabeth Gilbert

8. YOU WILL COME TO UNDERSTAND

Rest your thoughts in the
present moment, for fear and
anxiety do not reside there. Life
is full of change and the opportunity
for growth. There is a reason for
this life lesson.
You will come to understand.

FROM WHERE I STAND RIGHT NOW,
I'M BEGINNING TO UNDERSTAND THAT

MY SELF-GROWTH IS SHOWN IN

I don't care what the stars say about how small we are. One, even the smallest, weakest, most insignificant one, matters.

~ Rick Yancey
The 5th Wave

9. YOU MATTER

So much. To your children. To God.
To your friends and family.
To your community. To others you may help
as they go through this experience.
More than you can ever know.
You matter.

I AM LEARNING I MATTER IN
WAYS I DIDN'T SEE BEFORE

I AM APPRECIATED IN OTHERS' LIVES BECAUSE

Anger, resentment and jealousy doesn't change
the heart of others — it only changes yours.

~ Shannon L. Alder

10. YOU CAN FORGIVE AND LET GO

When you grow tired of the weight of
past hurts and resentments, let them fall off
your shoulders. Forgive yourself and others,
for as members of common humanity we are all
imperfect beings. Feel your burden lighten.
You can forgive and let go.

WHAT I STRUGGLE TO FORGIVE MOST IS

TODAY I BEGIN TO LET GO OF

There is a blessing hidden in every trial in life,
but you have to be willing to open your heart
to see them.

~ Unknown

11. YOU WILL FIND THE HIDDEN BLESSINGS

In this hardship. In the sleepless
nights and the heartfelt tears.
In the moments of reckoning. In the
trusted friends who are there for you.
Open your heart and mind. This life
lesson wants to serve you. You
will find the hidden
blessings.

I OPEN MY HEART AND MIND TO

IN THIS HARDSHIP I AM GRATEFUL FOR

So often in life the things you regard
as an impediment turn out to
be great, good fortune.

~ Ruth Bader Ginsburg

12. YOU ARE A PIONEER

Walking the road outstretched
before you, your destination unknown.
With faith in yourself, and a bright
and loving future. In carving a new path
with endless possibility.
You are a pioneer.

I'M CARVING MY OWN PATH BY

I HAVE FAITH IN MYSELF BECAUSE

You can actually create the life you want.
It all depends on how daring you desire it.

~ Lailah Gifty Akita
Pearls of Wisdom: Great Mind

13. YOU ARE A BELIEVER

In new beginnings. In your character
and what you're made of. In second
chances. In time as a healer of
all things. In the truth that events
do not define you. In the
knowing that you are the author
of your life story.
You are a believer.

THE STORY I CHOOSE TO WRITE ABOUT MY LIFE IS

I BELIEVE IN NEW BEGINNINGS BECAUSE

Sometimes you have to forget what you want, and remember what you deserve.

~ Unknown

14. YOU ARE LOVED

For your example. For your courage.
For being there for your children
when it mattered most. For the sister
or brother that you are. For being a good
friend. For your fortitude and
gentle humor. For being a child of God.
You are loved.

I AM WORTHY OF LOVE BECAUSE

I OFFER MYSELF COMPASSION WHEN

Someone once asked me how I hold my head
up so high after all I have been through.
I said, it's because no matter what,
I am a survivor. Not a victim.

~ Patricia Buckley

15. YOU ARE A SURVIVOR

Of life and its curve balls. With incredible
strength and fortitude. Designing
a life of hope, health, joy and love.
Manifesting your new vision for yourself.
You are a survivor.

SOME OF MY MANY STRENGTHS INCLUDE

THE NEW VISION I SEEK TO
MANIFEST FOR MYSELF IS

REFLECTIONS

REFLECTIONS

REFLECTIONS

REFLECTIONS

REFLECTIONS

REFLECTIONS

REFLECTIONS

REFLECTIONS

REFLECTIONS

REFLECTIONS

Jamie Daniel, MS, LMFT is a psychotherapist and owner at Life Connections Family Counseling in Westlake Village, California. Her practice is dedicated to helping individuals and families through the difficult transition of divorce through counseling, support groups and workshops.

Jamie travelled the personal journey of divorce recovery after the end of a 27 year marriage. Her experience was so profound, she has made it her passion to help support others experiencing the loss of divorce.

Jamie lives in Thousand Oaks, California. Her love and spiritual connection to the outdoors has her spending a lot of time on the local trails. She is the mother of three sons.

Please visit Jamie's blog, *A Whole New World: Chronicles of A Divorce Survivor* at chroniclesofadivorcesurvivor.com

Printed in the United States
By Bookmasters